How Do Video Games Affect Society?

Other titles in the *Video Games and Society* series include:

Video Games and Society

How Do Video Games Affect Society?

Patricia D. Netzley

ReferencePoint Press®

San Diego, CA

© 2015 ReferencePoint Press, Inc.
Printed in the United States

For more information, contact:
ReferencePoint Press, Inc.
PO Box 27779
San Diego, CA 92198
www.ReferencePointPress.com

LIBRARY OF CONGRESS CATALOGING-IN-PUBLICATION DATA

Netzley, Patricia D.
  How do video games affect society? / by Patricia D. Netzley.
    pages cm. — (Video games and society series)
  Includes bibliographical references and index.
  ISBN-13: 978-1-60152-748-6 (hardback)
  ISBN-10: 1-60152-748-9 (hardback)
  1. Video games—Social aspects—Juvenile literature. I. Title.
  GV1469.34.S52N47 2015
  794.8—dc23
                                                                    2014015008

Contents

Only a Game?

Games have been a human pastime for centuries. From simple dice and card games to increasingly complicated board games, they have provided hours of entertainment and a way to unwind from the stresses of everyday life. But with the advent of video games came different attitudes toward game play. Previously, social conventions dictated that adults play games only in certain situations—primarily at parties, after work was done, or while recuperating from an illness. But video gaming is typically viewed as something that can be done at any time, in any place.

According to research conducted by the video game industry, 35 percent of gamers play on smartphones and 25 percent on other wireless devices, which allows them to play wherever they are. In all, 58 percent of Americans regularly play video games, and 77 percent of them play for at least an hour a week. The average age of video game players in the United States is thirty; 68 percent of gamers are over eighteen, and 29 percent are over fifty. Men and women play in roughly equal numbers, though of the 47 percent who are female, most are over age eighteen. In addition, one-third of parents who play video games do so with their children at least once a week. Over 70 percent of parents believe that video games are good for their children, providing education and/or mental stimulation.

A Wide Variety

However, experts note that there are many different types of video games, and not all provide the same benefits. As an example of this variety, game company Big Fish produced 250 games in 2013 and offers fourteen different genres of games. This company specializes in casual games, a category encompassing games that have relatively simple rules and require little commitment of time on the part of the gamer. A puzzle game or word game that can be played while in a waiting room or on a work break, for example, would be a casual game.

In contrast, a hard-core video game is a game that encourages players to devote a lot of time to playing it, both during an individual gaming session and overall. These games are also generally more complex, with elaborate story lines that draw the player into the world of the game. Perhaps for this reason, hard-core games often develop a culture that includes competitions, conferences, and other events that connect game elements to the real world. Fans of hard-core games who immerse themselves in this culture might make lifestyle changes to support their game play and related activities.

According to some surveys, hard-core gamers often play in excess of two to three hours per day—or even more, if they have just obtained a new game. In such cases, they might play five or six hours or more at a stretch, possibly completing the game within forty-eight hours of starting it. Many gamers in the United States—both hard-core and casual—see nothing wrong with devoting so much time to a game. As gamer Ben Hill says, "One of the reasons we adopt entertainment as part of our lifestyle is to avoid that constant American rat race of being X-percentage productive and efficient in a given day."[1]

> "One of the reasons we adopt entertainment as part of our lifestyle is to avoid . . . being X-percentage productive and efficient in a given day."[1]
>
> —Gamer Ben Hill.

A Negative Impact?

Experts in the video game industry say that hard-core gamers not only devote more time to gaming but also spend more money than casual gamers. (Sales of video games and related hardware in the United States are expected to reach $24 billion in 2014; worldwide this figure is $76 billion.) Hard-core games also get the lion's share of attention from the media because some of them are extremely violent. Some experts say that playing games this violent makes an individual more prone to commit acts of violence in real life. Others, however, say that playing violent video games provides an outlet for aggression that actually reduces the likelihood someone will commit acts of violence in real life.

Experts also disagree on whether a passion for gaming is good for people. Even individuals who stick to casual games can become

The video game industry is big business. Sales of games and gaming-related hardware were expected to reach $24 billion in the United States and $76 billion worldwide in 2014.

so obsessed with their game play that they neglect other areas of their lives. In fact, studies suggest that video gaming can cause addictive behavior, and treatment centers have sprung up to address this problem. Avid gamers can exhibit antisocial behaviors as well, and they can experience physical effects, such as sore hands and obesity, from playing for hours at a time. But studies have also shown that playing certain video games can improve manual dexterity, hand-eye coordination, and mental-processing speed. In addition, games can encourage teamwork and provide gamers with a sense of community.

Nonetheless, whether the benefits of video gaming outweigh the costs remains a matter of dispute. Some people believe that certain types of gaming—particularly those promoting violence and/or antisocial attitudes—are harmful not only to individuals but also to society. Others argue that playing video games—even ones featuring violence or antisocial behavior—is no more likely to cause bad behavior than any other hobby. But researchers like Douglas Gentile, an associate professor of psychology at Iowa State University, take a more centrist approach. He says, "Playing video games is neither good nor bad. Existing research shows that they are powerful teaching tools, and therefore we need to harness that potential, aiming to maximize the benefits while minimizing the potential harms."[2] However, even experts disagree on how to do this.

"Playing video games is neither good nor bad."[2]

—Douglas Gentile, associate professor of psychology at Iowa State University.

Physical Costs and Benefits

It has long been known that playing video games can physically affect people in both positive and negative ways. Gamers who play for long stretches at a time often complain of hand and thumb pain, for example, even as they report improvements in manual dexterity. But scientific research into the physical effects of gaming is only just beginning to discover the depths of what this activity's costs and benefits might be.

Improved Cognition

Recent studies have focused primarily on the influence that playing video games has on the human brain. Many of these studies suggest that gaming can improve cognition, which is related to the brain's ability to acquire and understand knowledge. For example, in September 2013 researchers at the University of California, San Francisco (UCSF), reported that healthy adults ages sixty to eighty-five who played *NeuroRacer*, a three-dimensional (3-D) driving game designed for the study, for twelve hours over a period of one month subsequently demonstrated improved cognition and an increased ability to multitask. They also had better working memories and a greater attention span. Moreover, these improvements were still evident six months after the study concluded.

Neuroscientist Adam Gazzaley, who led the study, says that one feature of *NeuroRacer* was particularly important to improving participants' mental skills: as test subjects got better at the game, the game became more difficult. In this way, the game was training the brain to work harder—and as this occurred, researchers using MRI (magnetic resonance imaging, whereby a magnetic field and radio waves can create images of body tissues and organs) to view the brain saw changes in neural networks related to cognition. These changes made the neural networks look similar to those of much younger people, leading researchers to conclude that video gaming can reverse some of the negative effects of aging. Joaquin Anguera, who assisted Gazzaley in his work, says, "We see this as evidence that the training may have improved our study participants' ability to stay in an engaged, active state for a longer period of time"[3] than is normal for people of their age.

Another study showing improved cognition focused on younger people. Reported in November 2013 by the American Psychological Association (APA), this study found that 3-D first-person shooter games—hard-core games in which the player fires weapons from the point of view of a game character—can improve children's ability to think about objects in three dimensions and help them develop problem-solving skills. According to a 2013 report in the journal *Scientific American Mind*, several other studies have shown that first-person shooter games improve brain function, particularly in regard to decision making, learning, spatial reasoning, spatial focus, depth perception, visual acuity, and visual attention.

These improvements affect not only how well study participants play games as time goes on but on how well they perform tasks later in the real world. For example, one study at the University of Iowa showed that surgeons who perform laparoscopies—which are operations that insert a viewing tube through a tiny incision—make fewer errors if they have gaming experience. Another study at the University of California, Berkeley, showed that people with an eye disorder commonly known as lazy eye (poor vision in one eye primarily caused by underuse) experience a significant improvement in their condition after at least forty hours of playing a video game called *Medal of Honor: Pacific Assault*. Other studies have shown that even minimal first-person shooter experience can improve spatial reasoning and visual attention.

Bigger Brains

Researchers at the Max Planck Institute for Human Development and Charité University Medicine St. Hedwig-Krankenhaus in Berlin, Germany, have also found that playing certain video games can make brains bigger. In November 2013 they released the results of

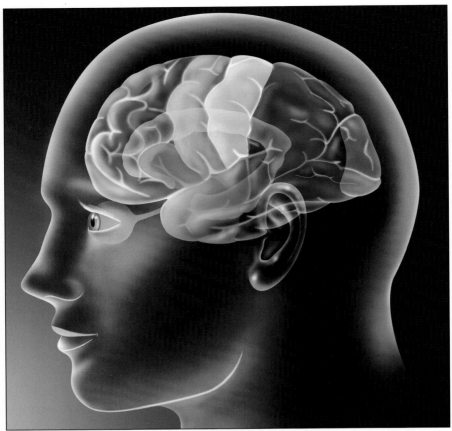

Many areas of the brain are activated while playing video games. The primary visual cortex (pink, rear), the primary auditory cortex (dark green), and the dorsolateral prefrontal cortex (light green, front) allow the brain to solve problems. The primary motor cortex (orange) and the primary somatosensory cortex (light pink, center) make it possible to work a joystick. The Broca's area (purple) is involved in speech, making it possible for players to communicate with each other.

a study that compared a control group of people who did not play video games with another group that played *Super Mario 64* for thirty minutes a day for two months. The researchers used MRI to study the brains of those in both groups. They discovered that the volume of gray matter in the brains of those who played *Super Mario 64* was significantly larger. Gray matter is the place where the cell bodies of nerve cells reside, and the areas of the brain affected—the right hippocampus, the right prefrontal cortex, and the cerebellum—are involved with spatial reason and focus, memory formation, strategic planning, muscle control, and fine motor skills.

Simone Kühn, the leader of the study, says that these results show that video games can train certain regions of the brain. Her research also shows that the more someone enjoys playing the game, the greater the increase in brain volume. She and her team believe this might be because the brain releases a compound called dopamine whenever someone is experiencing pleasure, and other studies have shown that reduced dopamine can lessen gray matter. In other words, perhaps the increase in dopamine is increasing gray matter.

New Therapies

The researchers also believe their work might eventually lead to game-play therapies designed to treat post-traumatic stress disorder, schizophrenia, neurodegenerative diseases like Alzheimer's dementia, and other disorders associated with the parts of the brain that are enhanced by gaming. One of Kühn's colleagues, psychiatrist Jürgen Gallinat, says that such therapies would be easy to implement. He explains that "many patients will accept video games more readily than other medical interventions."[4]

Other experts also find promise in the use of video gaming to cure mental disorders. In fact, in March 2014 UCSF opened a laboratory created to study whether and to what degree playing certain video games can help people with brain disorders. Gazzaley, the director of this facility, and his team of researchers hope that their work will result in video games being used someday as a form of therapy for people who suffer from attention deficit disorders and memory problems. They also speculate that video gaming might benefit people suffering from autism and the aftereffects of strokes.

Autism

Many parents of autistic children have reported that video gaming improved their child's thinking and social skills. One such parent, Liz Becker, comments on her son Matt:

> Being autistic meant that Matt was a loner—he didn't seem to like to play games. I believe the social interactions were just

too complex for him when he was little. Then we bought our first video game. It makes perfect sense that he would be so attracted to them. After all, the games were dynamic and visually appealing and he could play by himself. There are times when I have wondered if the real force behind his learning to read was the desire to know the rules, short cuts and to obtain all the bonus points offered in his video games.[5]

Becker reports that as Matt became more skilled at gaming, the activity became something that he and his older brother Christopher could do together, and playing with another person taught Matt how to deal with the frustration of losing. It also helped Matt understand that his worth as a person was not dependent on whether he could succeed at a particular task. In addition, figuring out the nuances of the societies depicted in games helped Matt figure out how to relate to people in the real world. Becker explains, "Games are not just games to the autistic child. To them they are a chaotic collection of mysterious mannerisms, facial expressions, voice fluctuations, gestures, and emotions that have to be unraveled slowly and meticulously to be understood."[6]

Sleep Disorders

But there is also a risk associated with encouraging autistic boys to play video games. In November 2013 a study at the University of Missouri, Columbia found that boys between eight and seventeen years old have difficulty falling and/or staying asleep if they keep computers or video game consoles in their bedrooms and play games before bedtime. However, those with attention-deficit/hyperactivity disorder (ADHD) had more trouble than boys without this disorder. The study also found that boys with autism spectrum disorder (ASD) had even more trouble than those with ADHD, receiving roughly 1.5 less hours of sleep per night than other boys.

While the study's researchers say it is unclear exactly what causes this, they theorize that in some cases it is due to the fact that children with ADHD or ASD can become overstimulated when playing video games. This can make it hard to fall asleep. In other cases, it might be that the screens of computers and other gaming devices are put-

Improved Vision

Although excessive gaming can cause eye problems, playing certain kinds of games in moderation can improve eyesight. For example, Daphne Maurer, director of the Visual Development Lab at McMaster University in Ontario, Canada, has discovered that gaming can be used to improve vision after cataract surgery for people who had been born with cataracts. Her test subjects, ages nineteen to thirty-one, played ten hours of the first-person shooter game *Medal of Honor* each week for four weeks. Some of them experienced improved vision within the first ten hours, and by the end of forty hours all of them had better eyesight and a greater ability to perceive small details and contrasts.

Maurer believes that these benefits are the result of playing a fast-paced game that combines the need for attentive vision with the need to take immediate action—also the conclusion of the work that inspired Maurer's study. Conducted by Daphne Bavelier at the University of Rochester in New York, this study compared eyesight changes in people with normal vision who played first-person shooter games with those who played *The Sims 2*, a life-simulation game that does not demand immediate action. Whereas the eyesight of the gamers who played shooter games improved significantly, there was no such change in the *Sims 2* players.

ting out enough light to disrupt the boys' production of melatonin, a hormone associated with sleep. Many children with ASD naturally have low levels of melatonin, which means they can ill afford a drop in production.

Other studies have shown that video games can affect the restfulness of sleep. That is, young people who play games before bed can wake up tired the next day even after getting eight or more hours of uninterrupted sleep. Research suggests that this is because certain video games can make players so tense that they remain on the alert even after they shut down the game. This means they are vigilant while sleeping—a condition common in primitive times when humans' survival depended upon the ability to sense the approach of predators while asleep. Vigilance makes sleep less restful.

Research has also shown that teenagers who play video games for more than fifty minutes before bedtime have problems falling asleep, to the point where some researchers have equated video gaming with consuming a caffeinated drink. (Caffeine can cause insomnia.) In a 2012 study by Flinders University in Australia, teenage boys who played violent video games for two and a half hours before going to sleep took thirty-nine minutes to fall asleep, experienced twenty-seven minutes of lost sleep during the night, and had twelve minutes less of rapid eye movement (REM) sleep, which is related to dreaming. According to the leader of the study, child sleep psychologist Michael Gradisar, "This may not seem like a significant reduction but REM plays an important part in helping us remember content we learnt that day so for adolescents in their final years of school who are revising [reviewing] for exams, winding down at night with a video game might not be the best idea."[7] Gradisar also reports that these gamers awoke frequently during the night.

> "For adolescents in their final years of school who are revising [reviewing] for exams, winding down at night with a video game might not be the best idea."[7]
>
> —Child sleep psychologist Michael Gradisar.

Physical Ailments

Playing video games can also cause eye problems, particularly if gamers do not take frequent breaks. These problems include nearsightedness (because a gamer spends so much time looking at something nearby: the computer screen), headaches, fuzzy eyesight, and a condition called computer vision syndrome (CVS). Perhaps the most common computer-related injury, CVS causes eyestrain, blurred vision, eye irritation, and light sensitivity. It can also be associated with neck and shoulder pain.

Other physical ailments plague gamers as well. One of the most common is pain, weakness, and/or numbness in the hand, fingers, thumb, and/or wrist, which can afflict gamers of any age. According to David Rempel, a professor at UCSF's Department of Medicine, using a gaming device that requires a lot of pinching or gripping poses particular problems in this regard, as do certain wrist positions and motions. However, the main factor in how much pain a gamer experiences is the number of hours of play. Those who play the longest tend to suffer the most.

In adults, hand pain is typically a symptom of carpal tunnel syndrome—the compression of a major nerve in the wrist and hand—but experts disagree on whether young children can develop this condition. Up until the advent of video games, it was typically seen in adults over the age of thirty. Therefore many experts believe that when pain in the hand or wrist occurs in young people who are heavy gamers it is more likely caused by muscle and/or joint distress from overuse. Such distress may lead to bursitis (inflammation of the bursae, which are fluid-filled sacs between bones, joints, muscles, and tendons) and tendonitis (inflammation of tendons, which connect muscles to bone).

A young boy stays up late playing games on his phone. Some studies show that young people who play video games just before going to sleep might feel tired the next day because their brains remain alert throughout the night.

However, many studies have shown that playing video games can also improve manual dexterity, the ability of hands and fingers to make coordinated movements, as well as hand-eye coordination. Gaming also has been used as physical therapy for stroke victims, providing them with ways to improve hand strength and grip as well as arm control. In addition, playing video games has been shown to reduce pain in burn victims and stress and fear in patients undergoing chemotherapy. Experts believe this is partly because gaming provides a welcome distraction for such individuals and partly because gaming releases endorphins in the brain, chemicals that can have a numbing effect.

Blood Clots

Nonetheless, experts caution that it is not good to spend too much time gaming without taking a break. This is because sitting too long in one position can cause neck, shoulder and back pain, especially when posture is bad. Another risk associated with sitting for long stretches is a blood clot. After too much time in a seated position, a person can develop a clot in the leg called a deep vein thrombosis, and if this clot travels to the lungs and becomes lodged there—a condition known as a pulmonary embolism—it can be fatal. Thirty percent of people who develop a pulmonary embolism die from it.

Twenty-year-old gamer Chris Staniforth of Sheffield, England, for example, died of a gaming-associated pulmonary embolism in 2011. Staniforth, who often played for up to twelve hours at a stretch, was sitting in front of his computer all night using Facebook and gaming. The next morning, while on his way to apply for a job, he collapsed after complaining of chest pains and died. Physicians say that had Staniforth gotten up from his chair roughly every hour to walk around a bit, this would have improved his blood circulation and might have prevented his death.

Obesity

Playing a video game for at least an hour at a stretch can also increase the likelihood that a gamer will eat more. A 2011 study by the American Society for Nutrition found that male teenagers who played video

Battling Dyslexia

Studies suggest that video gaming might one day be a common way to treat dyslexia, disorders that make it difficult to read. In 2013 researchers at the University of Padua in Italy were among the first to investigate this possibility. They placed children ages seven to thirteen into two groups. One played an action video game while the other played a calm one, with both groups engaging in nine gaming sessions of eighty minutes each for a total of twelve hours. Afterward both groups were subjected to reading tests and measurements of attention span. Researchers discovered that the group playing the action game showed significant improvement in reading speed and accuracy, but the group playing the calm game showed no such improvement. Moreover, the children who improved did so to a degree typically found after more than a year of conventional therapy for dyslexia. The researchers believe that such improvement is due to the way that active games require players to acquire, process, and react to information provided in the gaming environment.

games for an hour consumed more calories afterward over the short term than they did after resting for an hour. This was measured by providing them with a meal after play. However, test subjects did not report being more hungry or having more of an appetite after playing video games than they did after resting.

Experts disagree, however, on whether this increase in calorie consumption will result in obesity. Some say that it is obvious that excessive video gaming causes obesity since many gamers are obese, and indeed statistics show that there is a correlation between obesity and hours spent sitting in front of a television or computer screen. But according to the Kaiser Family Foundation, although the average amount of time that children spend in front of a computer screen increased two hours a day between 1999 and 2010, during this same period the number of obese children as a percent of population remained roughly the same. Moreover, a study conducted by Linda A. Jackson, a psychology professor at Michigan State University, found that statistically there is no correlation between obesity and screen time. The conclusion of her study states in part, "Although children may be spending more time at the screen, screen time is not responsible for the obesity explosion in America's youth."[8]

But if this is the case, what of the extra calories consumed by gamers? Some researchers believe the excess is burned off during game play. To examine this possibility, physiologist Arlette C. Perry at the University of Miami developed a study to measure the metabolic and physiologic effects of gaming on seven- to ten-year-old boys. She found that playing a video game increases oxygen consumption, blood pressure, heart rate, and the expenditure of energy as compared to sitting quietly. Perry's study results conclude that "playing video games . . . may not be a passive activity and may not have the same impact on the prevalence of overweight as watching television."[9] Perry found that watching television expended roughly the same energy as sitting quietly.

Exercise-Oriented Games

However, the amount of energy expended by gaming is not nearly enough on its own to reduce the weight of a gamer who is obese. Consequently, some people have suggested that gamers be encouraged to play exercise-oriented games like *Wii Sports* instead of games that do not require the gamer to move much. But studies have shown that exercise-oriented games are unsuccessful in combating obesity.

> "These games are not going to cure the childhood obesity epidemic. But they can be one useful tool, among many, in working toward that goal."[11]
>
> —Exercise scientist Bruce Bailey.

For example, a 2012 study by the Children's Nutrition Research Center at Baylor College of Medicine in Houston, Texas, and the Institute of Human Performance at the University of Hong Kong found that over a three-month period, playing an active video game did not reduce weight among children nine to twelve years old as compared to playing an inactive game. In fact, the study concluded that there is "no reason to believe that simply acquiring an active video game . . . provides a public health benefit to children."[10]

Another study, conducted by the University of Auckland in New Zealand, the University of Western Ontario in Canada, and

Teenagers at a Japanese arcade do the steps to Dance Dance Revolution. *Researchers say movement games such as this one provide moderate to brisk exercise.*

the George Institute for International Health in Sydney, Australia, found that obese and overweight children lost only a pound on average after six months of playing exercise-oriented video games. However, researchers at Brigham Young University in Provo, Utah, found that the games *Wii Sports Boxing, Dance Dance Revolution, LightSpace, Cavix, Cybex Trazer*, and *Sportwall* qualified as moderate to brisk exercise and could replace walking on a treadmill as a way to keep fit. Therefore, says exercise scientist and study leader Bruce Bailey, "These games are not going to cure the childhood obesity epidemic. But they can be one useful tool, among many, in working toward that goal."[11]

Many people agree that exercise-oriented games are useful when it comes to staying physically fit. So video game companies continue to develop more offerings in this genre, which is typically called exergaming. Some companies are working to create exergames that can be provided via smartphones so that players can exercise while outdoors. Among these games are ones that use GPS (global positioning system) technology to acquire information about the game player's environment so that the world depicted in the game will match the real-world features surrounding the player.

Other game developers are working to create games that exercise the mind to promote brain fitness. Some of these are being specifically designed for seniors by experts in brain science. In discussing such work, Jason Allaire, an associate professor in the Department of Psychology at North Carolina State University in Raleigh, says, "Whether it's a specially manufactured game or something like 'World of Warcraft,' games are cognitively complex and require mental energy and abilities to play them. Whenever you do anything that requires mental energy, you're exercising your abilities—it's just like if you exercise your muscles, you get stronger."[12] Some experts say that ongoing research will eventually lead to games that work both the brain and the body to promote overall physical health. If this is the case, then the physical benefits of gaming might one day far exceed the costs.

> "Whenever you do anything that requires mental energy, you're exercising your abilities—it's just like if you exercise your muscles, you get stronger."[12]
>
> —*Jason Allaire, an associate professor of psychology at North Carolina State University.*

Social Costs and Benefits

Chapter Two

Video gaming can affect people not only physically but also psychologically, influencing the way gamers interact with one another and with their communities in both the gaming world and the real world. Some of these social effects are positive, some negative. For example, as hard-core gamers form deep personal relationships online with fellow gamers, they can learn how to develop such relationships offline as well. Alternatively, they can decide to isolate themselves from the physical world so they can immerse themselves more fully in their online one.

Isolationism

Isolationist behavior primarily occurs among people who have difficulty limiting the amount of time they spend gaming. For these gamers, says David Walsh of the National Institute on Media and the Family, "Time becomes irrelevant. For some people, this is the center of their lives."[13] Such individuals tend to lose interest in school and work, and they have no interest in forming new offline friendships. If they have families, they may spend little time with their spouses and children. For example, in speaking of her husband, who spent up to eighteen hours a day playing video games, Sherry Myrow of Toronto, Canada, says, "I only saw happiness in his eyes if he was playing the game or talking about the game. The game consumed his life, and there was no room for me."[14]

Psychology professor Laura Walker of Brigham Young University in Utah, who has studied how gaming affects relationships, says that in the case of teens, video gaming can either prevent friendships from forming or serve as a comfort for someone who has no friends. She explains, "It may be that young adults remove themselves from important social settings to play video games, or that people who already struggle with relationships are trying to find other ways to spend their time. My guess is that it's some of both."[15]

Walker has also found that excessive gaming damages relationships with loved ones and lowers self-esteem. In addition, students who play video games daily smoke marijuana twice as much as casual players and three times more than students who never play video games, a behavior she considers harmful. "Everything we found associated with video games came out negative,"[16] she says.

Other researchers, however, insist that video games are a positive influence when it comes to relationships. Their studies suggest that gaming can draw people together, enhance a sense of community among players, and make them more outgoing and comfortable among others. For example, Cheryl Olson, who has studied the ways in which media can change behavior, says, "Video games clearly create a common ground that young people can use to make friends."[17] Indeed, according to a 2013 report by an APA task force studying the positive effects of gaming, more than 70 percent of gamers play with a friend.

> "Video games clearly create a common ground that young people can use to make friends."[17]
>
> —Cheryl Olson, an expert on how video games can change behavior.

This appears to be particularly true for teenage boys. Jennifer L.W. Fink, founder of the website BuildingBoys.net, which is devoted to promoting physical and psychological health for boys, notes, "Consider the fact that video games are a huge part of boy culture. When researchers ask boys why they play games, a large proportion of them say that the gaming is something to do with friends. Boys bond over games, in much the same way boys throughout time have bonded over sports teams and TV shows."[18]

Causing Depression

Most experts agree that video gaming can provide emotional benefits, including a sense of belonging, a reduction in anxiety, and an emotional resilience born out of learning to deal with losing. But Isabela Granic, the leader of the APA task force, says that people should not ignore the most obvious positive result of gaming: "If playing video games simply makes people happier, this seems to be a fundamental emotional benefit to consider."[19]

Sometimes, however, what begins as a happy experience turns into an unhappy one. This might be because a player's choice of gaming community proves to be a bad fit, or it might be because a player becomes

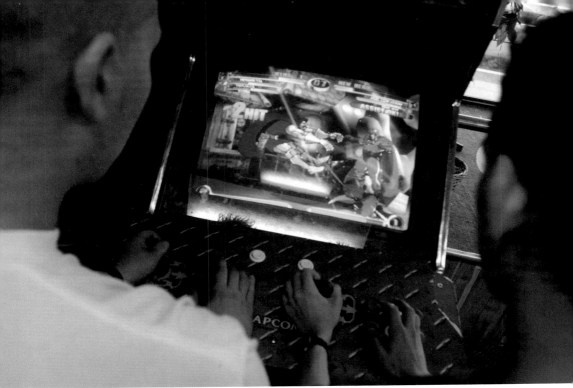

Two teen boys pit their gaming skills against each other. Most boys who play video games say they consider gaming something fun they can do with friends.

frustrated with a game and/or disappointed with his or her inability to stop playing it. As one gamer, Evan, complains in response to an Internet question on gaming happiness, "When I keep dying or losing in a game I get unhappy and start to rage but then I think to myself 'wait, why am I getting mad over a video game?' But when I do game, I feel really lonely and sad about myself because I could be doing other things like hanging out with my friends but instead I chose to play a game."[20]

Indeed, studies have shown that excessive gaming can cause depression. For example, in one two-year study of third-, fourth-, seventh-, and eighth-graders in Singapore led by Douglas Gentile, children who played an average of thirty-one hours a week, as opposed to those who played nineteen hours or less a week, were much more likely to suffer from depression and anxiety and to display fearful behaviors. About these findings, Gentile says, "I was expecting to find that the depression led to gaming. But we found the opposite in that study. The depression seemed to follow the gaming."[21] He adds that when the gaming stopped, the depression went away.

There have been few other studies into this issue. However, anecdotal evidence suggests that depression and heavy gaming can be so closely tied that it is difficult if not impossible to tell which one, if either, causes the other. This is the position of gamer Phil Owen, who had his own experience with gaming and depression. He recalls, "When I lost my job . . . I struggled immensely. For the next few weeks, I would spend an hour or so a day looking for more work, while devoting the rest of my day to playing *Star Wars: The Old Republic*. It was absurd and definitely out of the ordinary for me, but I was depressed. That's how I dealt with it."[22]

Owen tried to kill himself. However, he says that the game did not make him suicidal. Without it, he insists, he would have simply turned to some other potentially destructive way to deal with his emotional pain, such as excessive drinking. But others do believe that gaming drove their loved ones to suicide. This is the case with the mother of twenty-year-old Shawn Woolley, who quit his job so that he could play the fantasy role-playing video game *EverQuest* more often. After he killed himself while playing the game, Liz Woolley said, "That's how strong that game is. You can't just get up and walk away."[23]

Easing Depression

Nonetheless, certain types of video games appear to ease depression. For example, in 2012 researchers in New Zealand developed a 3-D fantasy game called *SPARX* and tested it on 187 young people ages twelve to nineteen with depression. *SPARX* is an acronym for *Smart, Positive, Active, Realistic, and X-Factor Thoughts*, which are terms derived from traditional approaches to treating depression. Half of the teens were treated by traditional means, typically one-on-one counseling, while the other half played the video game, which involved destroying negative thoughts to set the world of the game right. With each of the seven game levels came additional strategies for coping with negative thoughts. After a period of four to seven weeks of gaming, depending on how fast a player went through the levels, roughly 44 percent of the gaming participants had no more signs of depression, while only 26 percent of the nongaming participants did.

Another game that appears to ease depression is *Depression Quest*, during which players make decisions to navigate successfully through a life with realistic features of depression. One player, twenty-six-year-old Zoe Quinn, says this game helped her learn how to deal with her panic attacks. She says that in addition to the coping mechanisms she learned, "being able to jump into this digital world for a while, and not be stir crazy, was actually super helpful."[24]

Elizabeth Woolley holds a photograph of her son Shawn, who killed himself at the age of twenty. Woolley blames her son's death on his addiction to the video game EverQuest.

Gamification

Certain aspects of video games encourage people to work harder and longer to complete tasks in the virtual world than they might in the real world. When these same features are used to create game-like behavior in the real world, it is known as gamification. Gamification often harnesses people's competitive nature and their desire for rewards. For example, a company might use a system of reward points and achievement levels to motivate employees to compete with one another in accomplishing certain tasks. Gamification is also used to encourage people to dedicate themselves to solving complex problems. Perhaps the foremost example of this is *FoldIt*, an online puzzle video game invented by the University of Washington's Center for Game Science in collaboration with the university's Department of Biochemistry as a way to enlist the public's help in solving scientific puzzles related to disease prevention and treatment. As a result of this game play, over the course of just ten days in 2011—when the site had more than 240,000 registered users—players came up with key information on the structure of an AIDS-causing virus that scientists had been trying to unlock for more than a decade.

Therapist Lindsay Dobson also finds video games to be a helpful way for teens who are grieving to cope with their depression. Consequently, she incorporates gaming into her therapy sessions. She reports,

> If they're feeling angry they might come in and go onto a game that's violent. If they're feeling really boxed in they might go onto *Minecraft* and build a tiny room and lock themselves in it. They might say they've been on *Second Life* or *World of Warcraft* and they'll talk to me about what they've been doing on there. We explore the character they've chosen and why they've chosen to be that character.[25]

Different Games, Different Results

Many experts say that whether gaming has positive or negative effects on a person's behavior and/or thinking depends heavily on the game being played. For example, as reported by the APA, one long-term study reported in 2013 found that the more teenagers played strategic video games, particularly role-playing games, the more their school grades and problem-solving abilities improved the following year. Another long-term study, reported by Gentile, found that children who played prosocial games subsequently behaved in more prosocial, helpful ways. Gentile says, therefore, "If content is chosen wisely, video games can actually enhance some skills. But overall, the research has demonstrated that they're far more powerful teaching tools than we imagined. But the power can be both good and bad."[26]

As an example of the bad effects that a particular type of game can have, a study in Italy led by psychologist Alessandro Gabbiadini found that playing a violent video game for just thirty-five minutes led gamers to exhibit a lack of self-control, an increase in aggressive behavior, and a greater tendency to cheat. The researchers assigned study participants—172 high school students—to one of two groups. The members of one group played a nonviolent game (*Pinball 3D* or *Mini Golf 3D*), while members of the other group played a violent game (*Grand Theft Auto III* or *Grand Theft Auto San Andreas*).

Before gaming, a bowl of M&M candies was placed near each participant, and each was told that although it was fine to eat the candies, it was best not to eat too many too quickly. After the gaming, researchers measured the amount of candy eaten and discovered that teens who had played a violent game ate more. Researchers then subjected participants to tests related to morals. In one of the morals tests, participants were asked whether they disagreed with various statements, such as ones suggesting it was relatively harmless to shoplift or insult someone. The answers of those who had played a violent game indicated that they were more likely to find immoral behavior acceptable.

In another test, participants were given logic problems to solve and an envelope filled with raffle tickets. After they finished the prob-

> "If content is chosen wisely, video games can actually enhance some skills."[26]
>
> —Douglas Gentile, a researcher with Iowa State University.

lems they were provided with the correct answers and told to award themselves a raffle ticket for each correct one. Later the researchers compared the number of tickets taken from the envelopes with the number of logic problems solved correctly and discovered that far more of the teens who had played a violent game took more tickets than they deserved. Similarly, in a final test to measure aggression, participants were allowed to decide whether to blast someone else with a loud, unpleasant noise delivered through headphones, and the teens who had played the violent video game delivered such blasts more often and for a longer duration.

The researchers also discovered that teens who already had difficulties behaving ethically were much more likely than others to be adversely affected by violent video games. Specifically, those teens who were high in moral disengagement—the process whereby people rationalize their own unethical, unjust, or immoral behavior—were far more affected by their violent gaming than those low in moral disengagement. The researchers concluded that because the teens reacted differently depending on their moral makeup, it is unwise to base conclusions regarding the consequences of violent gaming on whether a particular effect is or is not present. Instead, studies should look at whether those effects are strong or weak.

Game Transfer Phenomena

Another game-related effect that varies in degree is game transfer phenomena (GTP). Researchers at Nottingham Trent University in the United Kingdom and Stockholm University in Sweden have jointly studied these phenomena, and they report that GTP occurs when certain events or aspects of real life trigger thoughts, sensations, and/or actions that are linked to a particular video game. The researchers call this a mental hiccup, whereby people act in the real world as they would in a game and sometimes perceive the real world as being part of the game world. One of the researchers, Angelica B. Ortiz de Gortari, explains, "GTP can be triggered by the association between real life stimuli and video game elements, resulting in subsequent automatic mental processes, altered perceptions (e.g., visual, auditory), involuntary or voluntary behaviours influenced by video games."[27]

Online Helpers

Among the positive aspects of online gaming is the fact that it can provide a lifeline for people who live alone and do not have a strong real-life social network—and sometimes this lifeline literally saves lives. As an example, a Canadian teenager became disturbed by the suicidal comments of a boy he was playing with and contacted police, who then contacted the makers of Xbox Live, the gaming system the boy was using, to find out where he was located and get him help. Similarly, a man with muscular dystrophy was playing an on-line game when a fire broke out. Physically unable to reach a phone or escape his house, he gave fellow players his address (not recommended under normal circumstances) and they contacted authorities for him. In another case, a man was driving behind an SUV when it swerved, flipped over, and starting spewing smoke. He rushed to help the bleeding victim, pulling him from the wreck and administering first aid using knowledge he had learned from playing a video game in which his gaming character was an army medic.

The mildest forms of GTP involve the reflexive use of a game action while performing tasks in the real world, such as when a car starts to skid and the driver automatically turns the steering wheel the way he would in a driving game. As another of the researchers, psychologist Mark Griffiths, reports, "Most of the experiences were neutral and often quite positive. We distinguished between what we call automatic GTP, which are almost like reflexes or classically conditioned responses, and those where players deliberately take elements out of the game and work them into their day-to-day routines."[28] People who reported experiencing these types of GTP generally view them as helpful. For example, some have employed strategies learned in the world of a game to succeed at real-life games like laser tag or have adopted the speaking style of a game character in order to interact more effectively with real-life friends or co-workers.

Other types of GTP are more complex, changing someone's perception of what is real and what is not. For example, a person who drops something in the real world might reach for a nonexistent tool that would be used to retrieve the dropped object in the game world, momentarily believing that the tool will be there or even hallucinating that it is there. Griffiths reports that

> the academic literature [on these phenomena] goes back to 1993. There was a case of a woman who had auditory hallucinations; she just couldn't get the tune of the game she was playing out of her head—it was very intrusive. But what came out of our pilot research were lots of different experiences, some that were auditory, some visual and some were tactile.[29]

Many physicians consider such hallucinations a sign that the gamer might be developing psychosis, a mental illness whose symptoms also include delusions, paranoia, and disorganized thinking. However, within weeks of ending all gaming, the hallucinations typically end as well. Physician Victoria Dunckley, who has treated sufferers of gaming-related hallucinations, theorizes that the reason for this has to do with the dopamine produced in the brain during gaming, which can lead to such psychotic symptoms as voices and delusions.

However, this would not account for GTP that are little more than memories of game play. An example of this is a phenomenon first seen in 1996 among players of the game *Tetris*. After playing the game for hours, some *Tetris* players would continue to visualize its falling blocks long afterward. As technology writer and editor Sally Adee explains, "Play long enough and you could encounter all sorts of strange hallucinatory residuals: some reported witnessing bathroom tiles trembling, for example, or a floor-to-ceiling bookcase lurching down the wall. In less extreme but far more common cases, people saw moving images at the edge of their visual field when they closed their eyes."[30]

Beneficial Results

Ortiz de Gortari stresses that such visions are not the hallucinations symptomatic of mental illness. They are a normal though relatively uncommon aspect of gaming that needs to be understood, not feared. As to how this understanding might help gamers, Griffiths explains

A video racing game offers a chance to test one's driving skills. Some research suggests that motor skills and reflexes can benefit from practicing driving maneuvers and other actions in video games.

that "some people may be worried that they're seeing things, but if they know it's a fairly normal phenomenon with no long lasting effects it might make them feel better. If we find in our future research that GTP is mostly experienced by intensive game players, we may be able to set time limits in order to stop the effects from happening."[31]

Griffiths also notes that research into GTP shows how learning something in a video game can help individuals and society, as with the driver dealing with the skid who saves himself and others from a possibly disastrous accident because he learned what to do by playing a video game. About this type of learning, Griffiths says,

If you're in a game and doing something repetitively, you're using the controls automatically, in the same way as an experienced driver can do it almost instinctively. So if you come out of the game and come across a similar situation in real life, this conditioned response kicks in for a second or two. From our interviews [with people who have experienced this] it's clear that gamers fully realise they're not in a video game—they're just taken back to it.[32]

Teaching and Motivating

In addition to teaching driving maneuvers and other skills through repetition, video games can also teach complex concepts and provide information in more engaging ways than traditional means of education can. For example, *Immune Attack,* a 3-D interactive video game created by the Federation of American Scientists (FAS) in 2008, has been used to teach high school students about the immune system. According to Henry Kelly, former president of the FAS, with such games, "the goal is to hook you. You can reach people who think they hate the subject. The minute you get swept up in the thing, you sort of forget that you hate science."[33]

Biology teacher Netia Elam, who tested the game in her classroom, was pleased with the results. She comments on the students who tried the game: "[With textbooks] they might read something, drag vocabulary words onto paper, or use their math, but they're not really integrated into it. Because they are playing video games, they were really engrossed in what they were doing. They took on more of an interest and more of an initiative to pay attention."[34]

Other educators, however, are reluctant to embrace the use of video games in the classroom. Kelly does not fault them for this. He says, "The teachers are right to be skeptical. There is concern that it's going to be distracting and a waste of time."[35] Nonetheless, US president Barack Obama has called on educators to develop compelling video games that will improve science, technology, engineering, and math (STEM) skills in young people. Consequently, experts are currently studying ways in which video games can be successfully integrated into classrooms.

Among those experts are Kurt Squire and Dennis Ramirez, who say that while current educational games are innovative, the future will likely bring offerings that are even more creative, providing "compelling experiences, learning through failure, exploration, collaboration, and construction." Squire and Ramirez add, "In our vision of [a] game-based learning future, kids are not only tethered to screens, but also physically and socially engaged in the world."[36]

In speaking of such visions, game designer Tadhg Kelly says that most people believe that video games hold great promise. "Growing up in the age of computers and technology and watching games grow up, we can almost taste it," he states. "We don't just like to play video-games, we like to imagine how they might influence society."[37] However, he doubts that this promise will be fulfilled, and he questions whether it should be. He considers the current state of gaming to be as good as it needs to be. But others argue that more can and should be done to turn gaming into a way to bring out the best in individuals to benefit society as a whole.

Video Game Addiction

Chapter Three

For some people, video gaming is a hobby easily set aside when another activity presents itself. But others feel compelled to play video games even when it is contrary to their best interests. For example, twenty-one-year-old student Ruya Cunningham (not her real last name) from South Carolina says of her passion for *World of Warcraft*, a game that requires players to assume the roles of mystical characters such as trolls and dragons, "Before [*World of Warcraft*], I had a job. I worked out every day. I kept my room clean. I got my nails and hair done. I took care of myself. That all changed when I became addicted."[38]

What Is Addiction?

Some experts, such as science and technology journalist Jack Flanagan, believe it is appropriate to call an obsession with video gaming an addiction because it has the same effects on a person's life as a physical addiction to substances like drugs and alcohol. He states, "Video game addiction exists. It has all the features you need to classify an addiction."[39] These include destroying one's relationships, health, and job prospects because of excessive gaming. It also includes an inability to stop gaming despite such problems.

> "I had a job. I worked out every day. I kept my room clean. I got my nails and hair done. I took care of myself. That all changed when I became addicted."[38]
>
> —Twenty-one-year-old student Ruya Cunningham on her addiction to playing World of Warcraft.

Other experts, however, argue that the word *addiction* should be used only to refer to the loss of control caused by a physical substance, as opposed to a behavior. One such expert is Jackson Toby, emeritus professor of sociology at Rutgers University in New Jersey. He says that video games are nothing but "strong temptations," not true addictions, and states emphatically, "I don't believe that someone can be addicted to video games."[40]

The position of people like Toby is based on the fact that although psychological factors might drive people to try substances like drugs or alcohol to begin with, physical factors are what keep them hooked on the substance. This physical dependency is triggered by altered chemistry in the central portion of the brain. When this area is stimulated, it provides the body with pleasurable feelings because it is rich in chemicals that carry messages from brain cell to brain cell. Known as neurotransmitters, these chemicals include dopamine, serotonin, norepinephrine, and endorphins, all of which affect emotions. Someone abusing a substance can develop a physical craving for these chemicals as well as a psychological craving for the pleasurable feelings they create.

Reward Systems

Some experts theorize that certain compulsive behaviors, such as gambling or video gaming, can stimulate the brain as well. If so, these

Two young gamers, one of whom is fast asleep, do an all-nighter at an Internet café in China. Video game addiction is like any other addiction; it can destroy relationships, health, and job prospects.

behaviors might become just as physically addictive as drugs or alcohol. Others say that even if video game addiction does not have a physical cause, its psychological causes are just as impossible to resist.

One such cause is positive reinforcement, a system whereby performing certain tasks results in specific rewards. In the game world this might include bonus points, special tools, or a promotion to a higher level of play. In any case, the brain soon learns to associate the activity with the positive feelings that result from being rewarded for that activity, and it develops the expectation that a similar reward might occur the next time the activity is performed.

> "Kill monster, get points. Complete level, get happy music. Win game, feel satisfied. It's a very simple and primitive part of who we are."[41]
>
> —Science and technology journalist Jack Flanagan.

Such associations and expectations provide a strong motivation to continue engaging in gaming behavior. As Flanagan reports, "How strong the reward system is in our brains depends on how often we get the reward and how big of a reward it is. Video games are built to exploit this part of our brain. Kill monster, get points. Complete level, get happy music. Win game, feel satisfied. It's a very simple and primitive part of who we are."[41]

A Sense of Community

In a 2013 study on the motivations behind addictive video gaming, Joseph Hilgard of the Social-Cognitive Neuroscience Laboratory at the University of Missouri, Columbia confirmed that the intermittent rewards provided within a video game can encourage addiction. But he says that other gaming elements can do this as well. This includes a sense of obligation to other players, which occurs when the game involves cooperative play. He explains:

> Players who are particularly excited by in-game rewards, such as time-consuming achievements and rare items, may find themselves compelled to play for excessive periods. Similarly, players who prefer games with a strong social component may find themselves more likely to become obligated to play the game, possibly leading to conflicts between game life and real life."[42]

The Most Addictive Game

Gamers disagree on which game deserves the title *Most Addictive*. Many would vote to place *World of Warcraft* in this position. But in March 2014 *Rolling Stone* magazine put *World of Warcraft* in the number-two spot, naming *Civilization* as the most addictive offering in video game history. According to Tom Hawking, who reported these choices,

> The addictiveness of these destroy-ancient-civilizations video games is more insidious [than other types of games]—it might be time for bed, but you promise yourself you'll just find the perfect place to found your second city, or quickly give Montezuma a much-deserved smackdown. And then you should probably find yourself a good source of copper, and decide whether to pre-emptively attack Bismarck, and . . . and then the sun is coming up and you're hunched over your computer, propping yourself up with an elbow as you repeat to yourself, "Just . . . one . . . more . . . turn."

His comments illustrate the thinking process associated with any addictive game, not just a civilization-destroying one.

Tom Hawking, "Game Never Over: The Top 10 Addictive Video Games," *Rolling Stone*, March 11, 2014. www.rollingstone.com.

Hilgard says that social games—games in which players have to work together to meet goals, gain rewards, and/or receive in-game resources—often make participants feel that they must play every day. A post in an online forum illustrates this sense of obligation. In writing to ask for help ending her mother's addiction to *Farmville*, a social game for members of Facebook, "Lilybelle1955" says that she could not convince her mother to quit because, in part, "my mother had found a bunch of other players on facebook to become friends with (in fact, they were writing and sharing with each other in a daily thread, which is still happening now—of course, we have never met these people) and she felt that if she stopped playing she would hurt their feelings."[43]

Farmville is what gaming experts call a massively multiplayer on-line game, so named because it involves a multitude of gamers connected to one another via the Internet. In the game's virtual world, players plow land, plant crops, and acquire items and animals for their farms. They can also gift each other items and sell harvested crops to one another. In this way, successful farmers have more connectivity to others than mediocre farmers, and this increases players' desire to tend to their farms, often to the point of addiction. As one *Farmville* player posted online, "You sit in your car with your laptop in front of the community college so you can use their wifi connection (which is faster than your broadband at home). So what if it's 30 degrees outside? I've got crops to harvest!"[44]

Another type of social game that is particularly addictive is the massively multiplayer online role-playing game (MMORPG). In these games players create characters such as trolls, elves, or dragons that represent them as they engage in shared fantasy role-playing in make-believe worlds. As a result, MMORPGs provide players with a sense of belonging to a unique community, although in this case it is a virtual community in which players have no face-to-face contact and do not know each other's true identities.

Some experts believe that this sense of belonging is the draw of MMORPGs. In addition, as with Lilybelle1955's *Farmville*-addicted mother, people become hooked on MMORPGs like *World of Warcraft* because it is a cooperative-play game and they do not want to let others in their social group down. This was the case with Ryan van Cleave, who wrote an autobiography entitled *Unplugged* to reveal his struggles with his *World of Warcraft* addiction.

But van Cleave did not play solely for the social connections. Other factors drove his addiction as well. One was the fact that in the virtual world he was a much more successful and powerful person than in the real world. In his book he explains that "playing WoW [*World of Warcraft*] makes me feel godlike. I have ultimate control

> "You sit in your car with your laptop in front of the community college so you can use their wifi connection (which is faster than your broadband at home). So what if it's 30 degrees outside? I've got crops to harvest!"[44]
>
> —A Farmville *player discussing his addiction.*

and can do what I want with few real repercussions. The real world makes me feel impotent . . . a computer malfunction, a sobbing child, a suddenly dead cellphone battery—the littlest hitch in daily living feels profoundly disempowering."[45]

World of Warcraft therefore gave van Cleave a way to escape from the real world. Flanagan says this is a common motivation because by playing, "people are escaping from their humdrum lives into a world of invented magic and wonder. This is why games like *World of Warcraft* are a gamers' 'drug of choice': they span massive worlds, across continents and with thousands of quests to join. If someone has a powerful imagination, the real world doesn't really cut it anymore."[46]

Other experts blame the addictive nature of MMORPGs on the fact that their puzzles and mysteries often take hours to unravel. Therefore, as psychologist Mark Griffiths explains, MMORPGs "are the type of games that completely engross the player. They are not games that you can play for 20 minutes and stop. If you are going to take it seriously, you have to spend time doing it."[47]

Playing to Death

Because MMORPGs require such a large investment of time, they are associated with some of the most extreme cases of gaming addiction. One such case involved a twenty-eight-year-old man in South Korea who was found slumped over his computer after spending what may have been seven days straight playing the MMORPG *StarCraft* in a 24-hour Internet café. Witnesses reported seeing the man taking breaks only to go to the bathroom, so authorities believe he ate little and went without sleep the entire week. Police later determined that the cause of death was most likely heart failure caused by extreme exhaustion. Similarly, a fifteen-year-old boy in Sweden suffered an epileptic convulsion after playing *World of Warcraft* with his friends for twenty-four hours straight.

But even when an addiction does not result in death, it can still be serious. For example, in describing her mother's addiction, Lilybelle1955 says that it caused her mother to become prone to anger and alienate herself from friends and family. The woman's anger was particularly severe whenever someone suggested she take steps to quit her game. Lilybelle1955 explains:

> If anyone ever wanted her to get away from the computer and stop playing Farmville, they were a horrible, horrible human being. The one time when I got up the courage to really try to talk to her about it and get it to stop, she lashed out at me, and the worst thing she said was, "Why do you want to take away the ONE THING that makes me happy?" I just couldn't believe my ears. My father, myself, our family, our animals, her photography, and any other thing she liked to do suddenly was . . . well, worthless to her, apparently. I backed off, realizing that I did not have the power to do anything about her addiction.[48]

An enthusiast of Farmville, the massively multiplayer online game developed for members of Facebook, creates a working farm. Players connect with each other as they build, run, and improve their virtual farms.

Getting High

This kind of behavior is not unusual among addicts. Hilarie Cash, a psychotherapist who treats patients with addictive behaviors, says that many people can become as hooked on video gaming as others become hooked on drugs. She says that most of her clients "have lost jobs, lost marriages, dropped out of college or high school, and their lives have fallen apart. They exhibit all of the standard characteristics [of addiction]. Their behavior is compulsive, they get a high off of it, they do it in spite of negative consequences."[49]

Cash adds that her clients have something else in common with people addicted to a substance: they need more and more of the object of their obsession to continue receiving the same level of satisfaction from it. She reports, "People will play . . . an hour of *World of Warcraft*, let's say, but then, after that, it's no longer making them high. They want more. And so they play more. And they develop tolerance over time. . . . Just over a matter of weeks and months, people can end up with a severe addiction."[50]

> "Playing WoW makes me feel godlike. I have ultimate control and can do what I want with few real repercussions."[45]
>
> —*Ryan van Cleave, on his* World of Warcraft *addiction.*

Going Through Withdrawal

Another similarity between a gaming addiction and a substance addiction is that when addicts do not have access to the cause of their addiction, they experience intense discomfort. With a substance abuser, this is because the body is no longer receiving the chemicals that satisfy the pleasure center of the brain. As a result, most people withdrawing from a substance abuse addiction experience nausea, vomiting, sweating, shakiness, and anxiety when the substance is withheld, an experience known as withdrawal. Depending on the nature of the addiction, the symptoms can last a few days or a few weeks.

Gaming addicts in withdrawal from their addiction can have physical symptoms as well, although some experts believe these have a psychological rather than physical cause. However, the majority of the symptoms are emotional. Cunningham, for example, experienced extreme anxiety when she was not gaming, and after she decided to uninstall the game from her computer to kick her gaming habit for good, she developed intense headaches and grew depressed.

Griffiths says that the presence of withdrawal symptoms is what separates addictive gaming from excessive gaming. As he explains,

> I've got very strict criteria that I use for video-game addiction: it has to be the most important thing in that person's life. . . . If you're unemployed with no partner and no kids and from the moment you wake up you play video games, and you play all day, that's not an addiction. Addiction has nothing to do with the amount of time you spend on something. If an addict is unable to play they'll get withdrawal symptoms."[51]

Therapy

Cunningham's depression eventually became so severe that she tried to take her own life by overdosing on sleeping pills. With the help of her parents, she sought professional counseling and was able to beat her addiction to *World of Warcraft*. "At least I am a person now, not an elf," she says, in reference to her gaming character. "I'm working on staying grounded in the real world."[52]

Whereas Cunningham needed one-on-one professional counseling to quit, van Cleave was able to quit on his own, stopping abruptly (known in addiction circles as *quitting cold turkey*) after he tried to take his own life. By this point he had lost his job and was on the verge of losing his marriage due to spending roughly sixty hours a week playing *World of Warcraft*. He had also gone into debt buying new computers and virtual-world game features that he felt would give him a better gaming experience. For cases this extreme, quitting cold turkey on one's own is not the norm; therapists who treat gaming addicts say that it is far more common for an addicted gamer to be forced by loved ones to seek help.

Various types of therapy are used to treat gaming addiction. Many of these are used to treat Internet addiction as well—that is, an addiction to online activities that might or might not include playing

An Unusual Cure

People have tried various means to cure themselves or their loved ones of a video game addiction. One unique approach was devised by the father of a twenty-three-year-old gamer in China named Xiao Feng. Feng had been working as a software developer for three months when he decided to quit his job so he could spend hours playing *World of Warcraft*. Upset by this behavior, his father hired several virtual assassins to kill Feng's character in *World of Warcraft*—not just once but whenever Feng created a new one. Because these assassins were at a higher level in the game than Feng, they were repeatedly successful in their goal. Nonetheless, Feng refused to quit playing, and eventually one of the assassins confessed that he was a hired gun. Feng then told his father that he would continue playing whenever he wanted and that he would find a new job when the right one came along and not before.

a game. One such approach is cognitive behavior therapy (CBT), a short-term therapy that helps people identify problematic thought patterns and change them for the better. The theory behind this approach is that thoughts and feelings can trigger behaviors but that people can end this cause-and-effect relationship. Patients are taught to recognize and try to avoid situations in which they are most likely to be tempted to engage in unwanted behavior.

In addition, therapists talk to patients about how they felt before having the addiction and about what feelings and circumstances led to it. Such discussions are designed to help patients avoid relapsing after kicking the addiction. According to a study by Internet addiction expert Kimberly Young, by the eighth session most of the 114 study participants were able to manage their addiction symptoms and sustain this management during a six-month follow-up period.

Treatment Centers

Whether CBT or another approach, therapy for a gaming addiction can be conducted one-on-one or in a group setting. Many patients choose to receive this therapy from a treatment center with experience in addressing gaming addictions. Such centers exist not only in the United States but in many other countries as well, including South Korea, China, the Netherlands, Canada, and the United Kingdom.

Most US centers use an outpatient approach, which means that patients come in for treatment during the day but go home again at night; treatment duration might be open-ended or it might be for a limited amount of time. For example, the Center for Internet and Technology Addiction in West Hartford, Connecticut, offers two- and five-day intensive outpatient treatment programs on Internet, gaming, personal device, and social media addictions, with each day lasting ten hours for the two-day program and four hours for the five-day program.

A South Korean teenager undergoes therapy to improve impaired concentration. The center where she is receiving treatment blames Internet and game addiction for this and other learning problems.

However, some people find it too difficult to quit gaming without removing themselves from the circumstances in which the gaming addiction was fostered. This is because one habit often triggers another. For example, someone who always plays *World of Warcraft* in a particular room might have a difficult time being in that room without thinking of *World of Warcraft*. A person with this degree of difficulty might choose to go into an inpatient addiction treatment center.

Such centers require the patient to live at the center for a period of weeks or months, completely cut off from all access to the sources of their addiction. For example, the Illinois Institute for Addiction Recovery in Peoria, Illinois, offers a six-week program of inpatient treatment during which gaming addicts have no access to video games. This center treats other kinds of addiction as well, which means that video game addicts might be in therapy groups with drug and alcohol addicts.

Some therapists say that the Illinois institute's approach is valid because all addicts deal with the same core issues. Others disagree, arguing that gaming addicts have unique issues that a one-size-fits-all approach cannot address effectively. With this in mind, some treatment centers specialize in video gaming. The first to treat gaming addiction only was a clinic in Amsterdam, Netherlands, established by Smith and Jones Addiction Consultancy in 2006. There are also treatment programs that specialize in treating teenagers, and these often combine addiction counseling with esteem-building exercises. For example, a ten-week program in southern Utah in a wilderness setting involves patients in outdoor activities.

Coping in the Real World

Experts disagree on whether this kind of isolation is the best way to treat gaming addiction. Some critics of inpatient centers, including psychiatrist Jerald Block, say that abruptly cutting off access to video games can be harmful if the addiction is being used to help the sufferer deal with difficult emotions that demand a gradual approach to ending the addiction. Other critics, such as Kimberly Young, say that isolation is unnecessary for successful treatment and presents an undue hardship for people who have jobs, families, or other responsibilities that demand daily attention.

In fact, until recently all treatment programs posed a hardship to those who could not afford them because insurance companies in the United States would not cover the cost of treatment. To be covered by insurance, a diagnosis of a particular disorder must be included in the *Diagnostic and Statistical Manual of Mental Disorders* (DSM), which is published by the APA for use by medical professionals, researchers, policy makers, insurance companies, and others. In May 2013 the APA decided to put video game addiction on its list of health problems that demand further study, and in January 2014 it decided that Internet gaming disorder is a valid diagnosis, similar to compulsive gambling—also in the DSM—because both involve impulse control problems.

This decision means that more video game addicts will be able to receive help with their problem—providing they can admit that they need help. It can often be difficult to convince someone that playing a game can be harmful, especially since it is so easy to lose track of time while playing. Many people have no idea just how long they are spending in the world of the game—until their real-world lives start to fall apart from inattention.

Video Games and Violence

Chapter Four

On July 22, 2011, thirty-two-year-old Anders Behring Breivik of Oslo, Norway, bombed a government building, killing eight people and injuring more than two hundred, then went to a summer camp for teens and opened fire, killing sixty-nine and wounding sixty-six before surrendering to police. Breivik's motives were political, but he later said that a first-person shooter game, *Call of Duty: Modern Warfare 2*, had helped him carry out his massacre. Having spent many hours playing, he decided to incorporate some of its details into his plans and was inspired to equip his gun with a holographic sight because of how well it worked in the game. In fact, he reported that had it not been for the holographic sight, he might not have been able to kill so many people.

Teaching the Wrong Skills

Critics of violent video games say that the Breivik case proves that such games are extremely harmful for society. They can train people to kill, these critics say, and give them ideas on how to do it on a grand scale and with great efficiency. As Breivik wrote in a diary entry from February 2012, "I see MW2 [*Modern Warfare 2*] more as a part of my training-simulation than anything else.... You can more or less completely simulate actual operations."[53]

Indeed, the military, police departments, and other law enforcement agencies have long used video games as a way to improve shooting skills, and studies have borne out the effectiveness of this approach. In one study at Ohio State University, just twenty minutes of playing a first-person shooter game made participants more accurate when firing at a mannequin. It also made them more likely to fire at the mannequin's head than at the torso. Brad Bushman, the coauthor of the study and a professor of communication and psychology, says,

"For good and bad, video game players are learning lessons that can be applied in the real world."[54]

However, experts disagree on whether these skills translate to real-world situations since firing at a target or a virtual character is different from shooting at real people. Journalist Paul Tassi, who has written extensively on video game issues, argues that "being good at Call of Duty makes you about as competent a soldier as playing Dr. Mario makes you a cardiovascular surgeon."[55] But Dave Grossman, a retired lieutenant colonel in the US Army, disagrees. He points to the case of a fourteen-year-old boy in Paducah, Kentucky, who shot at eight schoolmates and hit all of them, five in the head and three in the upper torso. The boy had experience playing first-person shooter games but no prior real-world shooting experience. Grossman states, "I train numerous elite military and law enforcement organizations around the world. When I tell them of this achievement they are stunned. Nowhere in the annals of military or law enforcement history can we find an equivalent 'achievement.'"[56]

> "For good and bad, video game players are learning lessons that can be applied in the real world."[54]
>
> —Brad Bushman, a professor of communication and psychology.

Desensitization

Grossman believes that in addition to improving a person's real-world accuracy with a weapon, first-person shooter games teach people that it is permissible to kill human beings. He says, "By sitting and mindlessly killing countless thousands of fellow members of your own species without any ramification or repercussions, we are teaching skills and concepts and values that transfer immediately anytime they get a real weapon in their hand."[57]

Other experts say that violent video games can desensitize players to death and violence. Desensitization is a process whereby a person is affected less and less by something as a result of repeated exposures to it. To determine whether violent gaming can cause this hardening of emotions, researchers with the Stress Research Institute at Stockholm University in Sweden conducted a study using two groups of thirteen- to fifteen-year-old boys. Half of these boys were accustomed to playing violent video games for three or more hours per day and the other half for an hour or less.

As part of the study, both groups of boys played a violent game for two hours before bedtime. Researchers then monitored their heart rates and evaluated the quality of their sleep. By bedtime all of the boys were exhausted from their game play, as though the violent gaming had worn them out. However, the researchers report that this exhaustion was not the kind that would encourage a good night's rest. Instead, it was an agitated, stressful fatigue that proved to negatively impact the quality of the boys' sleep.

But while none of the boys slept well, the boys who were less accustomed to violent gaming got worse sleep than the boys who were used to playing violent video games. The boys who were unaccustomed

A police officer in Sacramento, California, moves his virtual character through a hallway in a video game designed to train police in how to deal with a gunman who is threatening guests at a hotel. Video games such as this are considered effective teaching tools.

Video Games and the First Amendment

In 2011 the US Supreme Court struck down a California law that sought to ban selling violent video games to children. Specifically, the law would have made it illegal to sell or rent excessively violent video games to anyone under age eighteen, with the excessive nature of the violence judged by whether the game gave players the choice of "killing, maiming, dismembering or sexually assaulting an image of a human being" and was "patently offensive to prevailing community standards." However, Justice Antonin Scalia, in writing the majority opinion, said the California law violates "the First Amendment rights of young people whose parents (and aunts and uncles) think violent video games are a harmless pastime."

The First Amendment protects freedom of speech; in associating video games with this protection, Scalia equated them with works of literature and art. He explained,

> Like the protected books, plays, and movies that preceded them, video games communicate ideas—and even social messages—through many familiar literary devices (such as characters, dialogue, plot, and music) and through features distinctive to the medium (such as the player's interaction with the virtual world). That suffices to confer First Amendment protection.

Others, however, say that while video games might be protected, the extreme violence within some of them should not be, and there is no reason the government should not mandate that this violence be toned down or stripped out.

Quoted in Bill Mears, "California Ban on Sale of 'Violent' Video Games to Children Rejected," CNN, June 27, 2011. www.cnn.com.

Quoted in John D. Sutter, "The Court Sees Video Games as Art," CNN, June 27, 2011. www.cnn.com.

to violent gaming also had faster heart rates and were sad and anxious after their game play. "The differences between the two groups' physical and mental responses suggest that frequent exposure to violent video games may have a desensitizing effect,"[58] the researchers concluded.

They added, though, that boys who are drawn to play violent video games for three or more hours a day might have different traits than those who were light gamers, and these traits might have affected the study results. Still, other studies have seen a desensitization effect by monitoring the heart rate and galvanic skin responses (changes in the electrical resistance of the skin, an indication of emotional arousal) of people while they are exposed to violent images, both by playing violent video games and by witnessing incidents of real-life violence. In one such study it took only twenty minutes of playing the violent game *Duke Nukem* for test subjects to become less distressed at seeing real-life violence. Psychologist Craig Anderson of Iowa State University, who has conducted some of these studies, therefore considers video games to be highly effective desensitization tools.

Fantasy Versus Reality

Critics of violent video games say that in addition to causing desensitization, the most realistic games encourage players to believe that the world of the game is real. Grossman claims that up until the age of six or seven, children cannot tell the difference between fantasy and reality, and he argues that if they are overexposed to violence during this formative period, they will continue to blur the lines between fantasy and reality into adulthood. He says, "When the child spends more waking hours playing the game than he does anything else, what becomes fantasy and what becomes reality?"[59]

Henry Jenkins, a director of comparative studies at the Massachusetts Institute of Technology, counters that research does not bear out Grossman's position. In fact, he reports that even primates know the difference between violence associated with games and violence associated with real battles:

Classic studies of play behavior among primates suggest that apes make basic distinctions between play fighting and actual combat. In some circumstances, they seem to take pleasure wrestling and tousling with each other. In others, they might rip each other apart in mortal combat. . . . [For humans] the same action—say, sweeping a floor—may take on different meanings in play (as in playing house) than in reality (housework).[60]

But some gamers have said that it is not always easy for them to separate fantasy from reality. One is Evan Ramsey, who used a twelve-gauge shotgun to wound two classmates and kill another student and the principal at his Alaska high school in 1997. In a 2007 interview at Spring Creek Correctional Center in Seward, Alaska, he said that playing video games had made it difficult for him to understand what was real. He explained, "I did not understand that if I . . . pull out a gun and shoot you, there's a good chance you're not getting back up. You shoot a guy in [the video game] 'Doom' and he gets back up. You have got to shoot the things in 'Doom' eight or nine times before it dies."[61]

Causing Violence?

But even if games do blur the line between fantasy and reality, this does not mean they cause people to engage in violent acts. Whether violent video games cause violence is a separate issue from those related to players' perceptions and skills. It is also an issue that causes much disagreement.

In a 2013 analysis of ninety-eight independent studies on the connection between violent video games and aggression involving nearly thirty-seven thousand participants, Tobias Greitemeyer and Dirk O. Mugge of the University of Innsbruck, Austria, found ample evidence that such games do increase aggression and aggression-related acts. Conversely, playing prosocial video games increases prosocial behavior. The researchers also found that depending on the game and the duration of play, the effects could be both short term and long term.

Another review of studies completed in 2014 by researchers at Ohio State University found that in addition to raising heart rates and levels of aggression, playing violent video games decreased compassion toward others. A similar decrease in compassion was discovered as part of a study reported in February 2014. Researchers at the University of Illinois at Urbana-Champaign found that a player's selection of game character in the virtual world affects the player's behavior toward others in the real world. Someone who plays as a villain treats people in negative ways, while those who play heroes treat people well.

Students watch a fight between two high school girls. Some studies find ample evidence that violent video games lead to aggressive behavior.

Flawed Studies?

However, psychologist Christopher Ferguson, who has conducted his own research into the effects of violent video games, says that although many studies do seem to show that playing such games makes people more aggressive and more likely to behave badly toward others, these studies have often been flawed. He believes that many failed to take into account other variables, such as family violence or mental health issues. In addition, they typically did not give players enough time to become familiar with the game. That is, the duration of play was so short that players left the game frustrated that they were unable to perform well; in acting out this frustration, they exhibited more aggression than normal. Ferguson reports,

> Since . . . violent games tend to be more difficult to learn and have more complex controls than non-violent games, it appears that many participants in these experiments may simply have been frustrated by being cut off so quickly before they even learned how to play, rather than by the violent content of the game. Letting them play long enough to learn the game, or simply providing violent and non-violent games of equal complexity, erases the effects.[62]

Ferguson's own research has found no link between playing violent video games and becoming more aggressive. In fact, some of his studies suggest that video games, even violent ones, can actually make people more relaxed over time, thereby reducing aggression. This might be, he and others say, why statistics show that although sales of video games have gone up, youth violence has gone down.

Douglas Gentile agrees that there is no strong evidence that playing violent games leads to violent acts. But he says that this does not mean that violent games do not increase a person's level of aggression or that this aggression is harmless. He suggests that more needs to be done to investigate these games' effects on aggression as opposed to violence, explaining that

> the evidence that playing video games induces criminal or serious physical violence is much weaker than the evidence that

games increase the types of aggression that happen every day in school hallways. As a developmental psychologist, I care deeply about the everyday aggression (verbal, relational, and physical), whereas critics of the research seem to be mostly interested in criminal violence.[63]

Indeed, research suggests that teens who are exposed to violent video games will, over time, become more hostile, engage in more physical fights with peers, get into trouble more often with teachers, and generally do more poorly in school.

Media Influences

But just as discussions of video game research tend to focus primarily on criminal violence, so too do the American media seem bent on associating violent video games with criminal violence. Critics believe it is wrong to promote the idea that such an association exists. As journalist Tassi complains, "The media just refuses to let the notion go that video games somehow create violence, even though it's never been scientifically proven and 99.99999% of gamers who even play the most gruesome of titles do not end up killing anyone."[64]

Others have noted that in suggesting that playing violent games leads to being a violent person, the media ignore the possibility that violent people might simply be drawn to violent games. In calling attention to this problem, writer Julia Layton says,

> "The media just refuses to let the notion go that video games somehow create violence, even though . . . 99.99999% of gamers who even play the most gruesome of titles do not end up killing anyone."[64]
>
> —Journalist Paul Tassi.

Even an obvious relationship between virtual aggression and real-life aggression, like acting out the specific behaviors portrayed in [the violent video game] 'Grand Theft Auto,' isn't necessarily one of cause and effect. It may be that real-life violent psychopaths enjoy being virtual violent psychopaths, and they choose games based on that preference.[65]

Genetics and Violent Video Games

In February 2014 researchers associated with the University of Amsterdam's School of Communication Research reported that there might be a genetic reason for people to be drawn to playing violent video games. The Dutch parents participating in the study recorded how much time their children (ages five to nine) spent viewing violent television programs and playing violent video games. The latter included *Call of Duty* and *Grand Theft Auto.*

Meanwhile, the researchers analyzed DNA samples that had been taken at birth from all of the children. They discovered that the children who were the most compelled to view violent images had a gene that adversely affected the transportation of serotonin in the body. The researchers knew that a drop in serotonin can cause depression, anxiety, and aggression. They also knew that playing stimulating games can increase serotonin. From all of this information they concluded that the gene might influence excessive playing of violent video games.

Another study by German researchers in 2012 found a difference in the DNA of people who were drawn to using the Internet excessively and those who were not. These researchers theorized that this genetic variation changed the brain's reward system, thereby making Internet use more compelling.

Critics of reports on mass shootings also complain that in an attempt to make a stronger connection between playing violent games and becoming a violent person, the media fail to point out that it is statistically likely that any male in his teens or twenties, violent or not, will have experience playing violent video games. In fact, Patrick Markey, a psychology professor at Villanova University in Pennsylvania, reports that 97 percent of teens play violent video games. This means it would be unusual for the perpetrator of a school shooting, for example, not to be a gamer. Markey says, "It could similarly be argued that bread consumption predicts school shootings, because most school shooters likely consumed a bread product within 24 hours before their violent attacks."[66]

Nonetheless, the media are quick to report that the shooter was a gamer and repeat this fact often, making it appear extremely significant. Moreover, in their eagerness to blame violent video games for the deaths, the media often ignore the other activities of the shooter. For example, Adam Lanza, who killed twenty children and six adults in a school shooting at Sandy Hook Elementary School in Connecticut in 2012, had a video game collection that included the violent games *Call of Duty*, *Splinter Cell*, and *Mercenaries*, and the media reported on these. But what they often failed to mention was that Lanza had several nonviolent games as well, and he was particularly passionate about the harmless dancing game *Dance Dance Revolution*.

In complaining about how the media reported this story, technology expert Timothy Geigner says, "People that want to draw conclusions about Adam Lanza from his gaming habits don't get to cherry-pick their facts. If we're blaming the games that include violence, surely we must include the games that don't, particularly the game with which he was most obsessed."[67]

> "It could similarly be argued that bread consumption predicts school shootings, because most school shooters likely consumed a bread product within 24 hours before their violent attacks."[66]
>
> —Patrick Markey, a psychology professor at Villanova University in Pennsylvania.

A Complex Problem

Critics of the media blame such biases on people's desire to find a relatively easy way to prevent future acts of violence as horrific as the Sandy Hook shooting: if violent video games inspire school shootings, then banning such games will end them. But such a solution would also suggest that large numbers of people are potential killers. As Erik Kain, a gamer who also writes about gaming, explains,

> If it were as simple as saying "violent video games kill people!" then we'd really be in trouble. It's a silly fallacy, of course. (Homicidal maniacs kill people. Homicidal maniacs play video games. Therefore, video games cause homicidal maniacs to kill people.) If it were true, millions of your neighbors, kids, and co-workers would be violent killers. So far as I can tell, this is not the case.[68]

This is because other factors are at work in the making of a mass shooter. Psychological makeup, upbringing, and environment all play a role in whether someone commits a violent act. Recognizing this, Gentile asserts,

> I think it's the wrong question—whether there is a link between mass shootings and violent video game play. I understand people want to look for a culprit, but the truth of the matter is that there is never one cause. There is a cocktail of multiple causes coming together. And so no matter what single thing we focus on, whether it be violent video games, abuse as a child, doing drugs, being in a gang—not one of them is sufficient to cause aggression. But when you start putting them together, aggression becomes pretty predictable.[69]

Indeed, many studies have shown that people who commit mass shootings have serious psychological issues that go beyond anything that could possibly be associated with gaming. Most experts agree, then, that there is no way that playing a violent video game could turn a normal, healthy person into a mass murderer. With this degree of violence, there must be other influences at work.

The Sandy Hook shooting is a prime example of how many factors besides gaming experience can be involved in what drives a person to commit such a horrific act of violence. Before the shooting, Lanza's mother had long been worried about her son's mental health, although he was never diagnosed with a mental illness, and she had been speaking of having him committed to a mental health facility. He changed clothes frequently throughout the day, and his food had to be prepared and presented in a certain way or he became upset. He also became upset at loud noises, including the ringing of a doorbell; could not stand being touched; refused to sleep anywhere but his own bed; and had difficulty interacting with others. By the time of the massacre, he was refusing to communicate with his mother except by text message or e-mail, even though the two were living alone together in the family home. Nonetheless, his mother bought him numerous guns and often took him to a shooting range, and it appears that his passion for weapons far exceeded his interest in violent video games.

Members of the media gather for a press conference about the mass shootings at Sandy Hook Elementary School in Connecticut in 2012. The media often jump on video games as a possible influence on the perpetrators of high-profile shootings.

Lanza's actions on the day of the shooting also suggest mental disturbance. He shot every victim at the school more than once—a six-year-old boy was shot eleven times—and before arriving at the school he had killed his mother by shooting her four times while she was asleep in her bed. In a March 2014 interview, Lanza's father, who was divorced from his mother, said his son was evil and could just as easily have killed him as well had he been living in the same home. Adam Lanza killed himself shortly after police arrived at the scene of the shooting.

Violent Individuals

Because of these circumstances, many people say it is obvious that Lanza was a disturbed individual. Others say he was murderous rather than mentally ill. Harvard psychiatry professor Henry J. Friedman is among those who label such killers murderous individuals—sane but with a tendency to react to bad situations by committing murder. He adds that such people typically have a desire to die young in a cataclysmic way that attracts media attention.

Many experts doubt that a murderous state can be created by violent video games, just as they do not believe that a game can lead to a mental illness. However, studies suggest that certain people are vulnerable to suffering negative psychological effects from playing violent games. Those most deeply affected are individuals with personality traits that indicate they might have or be developing psychoticism, most especially a lack of empathy, nonconformity, and impulsiveness. Such individuals are prone to react to conflicts even when they have had no gaming experience. This means that the kind of violent acts that grab media attention are likely to be committed by people with violent tendencies unrelated to whatever games they might have played.

Meanwhile, most people who play video games do so without problems, complaints, or an urge to commit real-life violent acts. Violence is kept strictly in the virtual world, where, as Kain notes, "we can drive through stop lights, mow over civilians, crash and die and start over, get in ridiculous gunfights and still walk away on two feet. Or even just go shopping, or play golf, or hunt. We are given a vast canvas of possibilities, and the freedom to pretend to break bad in a cartoonish, outlandish, alternative reality."[70] Many of those who criticize violent video games may not realize just how enjoyable this activity can be, believing instead that such games can only be harmful to society, despite the fact that millions of gamers play without incident.

Source Notes

Introduction: Only a Game?

1. Quoted in Noah Nelson, "Gaming's Other Great Schism: Hardcore Versus Casual," *All Tech Considered* (blog), NPR, November 22, 2013. www.npr.org.

2. Quoted in Mike Ferlazzo, "Are Videogames Good or Bad . . . or Both?," Futurity, December 30, 2011. www.futurity.org.

Chapter One: Physical Costs and Benefits

3. Quoted in Laura Kurtzman, "Training the Older Brain in 3D: Video Game Enhances Cognitive Control," UCSF, September 4, 2013. www.ucsf.edu.

4. Max-Planck-Gesellschaft, "How Video Gaming Can Be Beneficial for the Brain," October 30, 2013. www.mpg.de.

5. Liz Becker, "With Autism a Game Is Not Just a Game," Autism Support Network. www.autismsupportnetwork.com.

6. Becker, "With Autism a Game Is Not Just a Game."

7. Quoted in Jeffrey Matulef, "Playing Games Before Bed Is Bad for You, According to Science," Eurogamer, October 23, 2012. www.eurogamer.net.

8. Linda A. Jackson et al., "Internet Use, Videogame Playing, and Cell Phone Use as Predictors of Children's Body Mass Index (BMI), Body Weight, Academic Performance, and Social and Overall Self-Esteem," *Computers in Human Behavior*, vol. 27, 2011, pp. 599–604. http://news.msu.edu.

9. Xuewen Wang and Arlette C. Perry, "Metabolic and Physiologic Responses to Video Game Play in 7- to 10-Year-Old Boys,"

Archives of Pediatric and Adolescent Medicine, vol. 160, no. 4, 2006, pp. 411–15. http://archpedi.jamanetwork.com.

10. Tom Baranowski et al., "Impact of an Active Video Game on Healthy Children's Physical Activity," *Pediatrics,* February 27, 2012. http://pediatrics.aappublications.org.

11. Quoted in Mike Fahey, "Can Video Games Keep Your Children Physically Fit?," Kotaku, March 8, 2011. http://kotaku.com.

12. Quoted in Drew Guarini, "9 Ways Video Games Can Actually Be Good for You," *Huffington Post,* November 7, 2013. www.huffing tonpost.com.

Chapter Two: Social Costs and Benefits

13. Quoted in David Zizzo, "Realities of Virtual Obsession," *Daily Oklahoman,* September 2, 2008. http://newsok.com.

14. Quoted in Zizzo, "Realities of Virtual Obsession."

15. Quoted in Julia Hoppock, "Playing to Learn: Video Games in the Classroom," ABC News, June 13, 2008. http://abcnews.go.com.

16. Quoted in Kurt Squire and Dennis Ramirez, "Video Games Take Learning to New Heights," Amplify, June 18, 2013. www.amplify .com.

17. Quoted in Jennifer L.W. Fink, "Who Says Video Games Are Anti-social?," *Parade,* November 4, 2013. http://parade.conde nast.com.

18. Fink, "Who Says Video Games Are Anti-social?"

19. Quoted in Rick Nauert, "Video Games Can Help Boost Social, Memory & Cognitive Skills," PsychCentral, November 26, 2013. http://psychcentral.com.

20. Quoted in Yahoo! Answers, "Do Video Games Make You Un-happy?," https://answers.yahoo.com.

21. Quoted in Phil Owen, "Do Videogames Make Depression Worse?," Kotaku, November 26, 2012. http://kotaku.com.

22. Owen, "Do Videogames Make Depression Worse?"

23. Quoted in *48 Hours*, "Addicted: Suicide over *EverQuest*?," CBS News, October 18, 2002. www.cbsnews.com.

24. Quoted in Jim Taylor, "Could Video Games Help to Beat Depression?," BBC, January 17, 2014. www.bbc.com.

25. Quoted in Taylor, "Could Video Games Help to Beat Depression?"

26. Quoted in Ferlazzo, "Are Video Games Good or Bad . . . or Both?"

27. Angelica B. Ortiz de Gortari, "Home," Game Transfer Phenomena. www.gametransferphenomena.com.

28. Quoted in Keith Stuart, "'Game Transfer Phenomena' and the Problem of Perception," *Games* (blog), *Guardian*, September 22, 2011. www.theguardian.com.

29. Quoted in Stuart, "'Game Transfer Phenomena' and the Problem of Perception."

30. Sally Adee, "Level-Up Life: How Video Gaming Can Enhance Your Reality," *New Scientist,* January 4, 2012. www.newscientist.com.

31. Quoted in Stuart, "'Game Transfer Phenomena' and the Problem of Perception."

32. Quoted in Stuart, "'Game Transfer Phenomena' and the Problem of Perception."

33. Quoted in Julia Hoppock, "Playing to Learn."

34. Quoted in Hoppock, "Playing to Learn."

35. Quoted in Hoppock, "Playing to Learn."

36. Squire and Ramirez, "Video Games Take Learning to New Heights."

37. Tadhg Kelly, "What Games Are: The Unfulfilled Promise of Video Games," TechCrunch, October 6, 2013. http://techcrunch.com.

38. Quoted in John DiConsiglio, "Game Over," *Scholastic Choices*, January 2008, vol. 23, no. 4. www.davis.k12.ut.us.

39. Jack Flanagan, "The Psychology of Video Game Addiction," *Kernel*, February 6, 2014. http://theweek.com.

40. Quoted in Tamara Lush, "At War with *World of Warcraft*: An Addict Tells His Story," *Guardian*, August 29, 2011. www.theguardian.com.

41. Flanagan, "The Psychology of Video Game Addiction."

42. Joseph Hilgard, Christopher R. Engelhardt, and Bruce D. Bartholow, "Individual Differences in Motives, Preferences, and Pathology in Video Games: The Gaming Attitudes, Motives, and Experiences Scales (GAMES)," *Frontiers in Psychology*, September 9, 2013. http://journal.frontiersin.org.

43. Lilybelle1955, "My Mother Is Addicted to *Farmville* & My Family and I Are Worried—Please Help!," Online Gamers Anonymous, August 27, 2011. www.olganon.org.

44. Quoted in Tim Martin, "*Farmville:* The Addiction," News Blaze, March 20, 2010. http://newsblaze.com.

45. Quoted in Lush, "At War with *World of Warcraft*."

46. Flanagan, "The Psychology of Video Game Addiction."

47. Quoted in BBC News, "S Korean Dies After Games Session," August 10, 2005. http://news.bbc.co.uk.

48. Lilybelle1955, "My Mother Is Addicted to *Farmville* & My Family and I Are Worried—Please Help!"

49. Quoted in *Talk of the Nation*, "Compulsive Video Gaming: Addiction or Vice?," NPR, July 10, 2007. www.wbur.org.

50. Quoted in *Talk of the Nation*, "Compulsive Video Gaming."

51. Quoted in Tom Meltzer, "I Was a Games Addict," *Guardian*, March 10, 2011. www.theguardian.com.

52. Quoted in DiConsiglio, "Game Over."

53. Quoted in Tom Law, "Anders Breivik: Did *Call of Duty* Really Influence the Norway Massacre?," *Sabotage Times*. www.sabotage times.com.

54. Quoted in Jeff Grabmeier, "Video Games Can Teach How to Shoot Guns More Accurately and Aim for the Head," Ohio State University Research Communications, April 30, 2012. http://re searchnews.osu.edu.

55. Paul Tassi, "The Idiocy of Blaming Video Games for the Norway Massacre," *Forbes*, April 19, 2012. www.forbes.com.

56. Dave Grossman, "Teaching Kids to Kill," Killology Research Group. www.killology.com.

57. Dave Grossman, "The Violent Video Game Plague," Knowledge of Reality. www.sol.com.au/kor/17_03.htm.

58. Quoted in GamePolitics.com, "Research: Frequent Exposure to Violent Video Games May Have 'Desensitizing Effect,'" May 10, 2013. www.gamepolitics.com.

59. Quoted in Ted Gregory, "Big Game Hunting: A Former Soldier and Expert on Killing Sets His Sights on Violent Video Games," *Chicago Tribune*, July 25, 2000. http://articles.chicagotribune .com.

60. Henry Jenkins, "Reality Bytes: Eight Myths About Video Games Debunked," *The Video Game Revolution*. www.pbs.org.

61. Quoted in Julia Layton, "Do Violent Video Games Lead to Real Violence?," How Stuff Works, January 2014. http://electronics .howstuffworks.com.

62. Christopher Ferguson, "Video Games Don't Make Kids Violent," *Time*, December 7, 2011. http://ideas.time.com.

63. Quoted in Ferlazzo, "Are Video Games Good or Bad . . . or Both?"

64. Tassi, "The Idiocy of Blaming Video Games for the Norway Massacre."

65. Quoted in Layton, "Do Violent Video Games Lead to Real Violence?"

66. Quoted in Layton, "Do Violent Video Games Lead to Real Violence?"

67. Timothy Geigner, "Lessons Learned from Adam Lanza's Video Game Obsession: Blame *Dance Dance Revolution*," *TechDirt* (blog), November 27, 2013. www.techdirt.com.

68. Erik Kain, "Do Games Like 'Grand Theft Auto V' Cause Real-World Violence?," *Forbes*, September 18, 2013. www.forbes.com.

69. Quoted in Layton, "Do Violent Video Games Lead to Real Violence?"

70. Kain, "Do Games Like 'Grand Theft Auto V' Cause Real-World Violence?"

American Civil Liberties Union (ACLU)

125 Broad St., 18th Floor
New York, NY 10004
phone: (212) 549-2500
e-mail: aclu@aclu.org
website: www.aclu.org

The ACLU opposes government efforts to censor books, movies, video games, and other forms of media and has been involved in many legal cases related to First Amendment rights.

Center for Internet and Technology Addiction

17 S. Highland St.
West Hartford, CT 06119
phone: (860) 561-8727
e-mail: drdave@virtual-addiction.com
website: www.virtual-addiction.com

The Center for Internet and Technology Addiction provides counseling, information, and resources related to online addictions. Its website offers articles, news releases, and videos related to these addictions.

The Center for Media and Public Affairs (CMPA)

933 N. Kenmore St., Suite 405
Arlington, VA 22201
phone: (571) 319-0029
e-mail: mail@cmpa.com
website: www.cmpa.com

The CMPA conducts research on how the media affect Americans and provides information on media-related issues.

Entertainment Software Association (ESA)

575 Seventh St. NW, Suite 300
Washington, DC 20004
e-mail: esa@theesa.com
website: www.theesa.com

A trade association, the ESA represents companies that publish and market video games and has been involved in legal efforts to fight the censorship of games and the restriction of their sales to minors.

Games for Change

261 Madison Ave., 9th Floor
New York, NY 10016
phone: (212) 242-4922
website: www.gamesforchange.org

A nonprofit corporation founded in 2004, this organization supports efforts to achieve social impact through digital games. To this end, it invests in game development projects that seek to leverage entertainment and engagement for the social good.

Illinois Institute for Addiction Recovery

5409 N. Knoxville Ave.
Peoria, IL 61614
phone: (800) 522-3784
website: www.addictionrecov.org

The Illinois Institute for Addiction Recovery provides treatment for all forms of addiction, including Internet and gaming addictions. Its website offers information related to these issues and provides access to the institute's online magazine, *Paradigm*, which contains articles for professionals and individuals interested in addiction-related subjects.

reSTART Center for Digital Technology Sustainability
1001 290th Ave. SE
Fall City, WA 98024-7403
phone: (800) 682-6934
www.netaddictionrecovery.com
reSTART offers an addiction recovery program for Internet and gaming addicts and provides information on how to use technology wisely.

Books

Tom Bissell, *Extra Lives: Why Video Games Matter.* New York: Vintage Books, 2011.

Lydia Bjornlund, *The History of Video Games.* San Diego, CA: ReferencePoint Press, 2014.

Neils Clark and P. Shavaun Scott, *Game Addiction: The Experience and the Effects.* Jefferson, NC: McFarland, 2009.

Andrew P. Doan and Brooke Strickland, *Hooked on Games: The Lure and Cost of Video Game and Internet Addiction.* Coralville, IA: FEP International, 2012.

Tristan Donovan, *Replay: The History of Video Games.* East Sussex, UK: Yellow Ant, 2010.

James Paul Gee, *Good Video Games and Good Learning.* New York: Peter Lang, 2013.

Dave Grossman and Gloria DeGaetano, *Stop Teaching Our Kids to Kill.* New York: Harmony, 2014.

Jesper Juul, *The Art of Failure: An Essay on the Pain of Playing Video Games.* Cambridge, MA: MIT Press, 2013.

Jane McGonigal, *Reality Is Broken: Why Games Make Us Better and How They Can Change the World.* New York: Penguin, 2011.

Kevin Roberts, *Cyber Junkie: Escape the Gaming and Internet Trap.* Center City, MN: Hazelden, 2010.

Constance Steinkuehler, Kurt Squire, and Sasha Barab (eds.), *Games, Learning, and Society: Learning and Meaning in the Digital Age*. New York: Cambridge University Press, 2012.

Internet Sources

Mary Bellis, "Computer and Video Game History," About.com Inventors. http://inventors.about.com/library/inventors/blcomputer _videogames.htm.

Doug Gross, "The 10 Most Controversial Violent Video Games," CNN, August 26, 2013. www.cnn.com/2013/08/26/tech/gaming -gadgets/controversial-violent-video-games.

Tom Hawking, "Game Never Over: The Ten Most Addictive Video Games," *Rolling Stone*. www.rollingstone.com/culture/pictures /game-never-over-10-most-addictive-video-games-20140311.

Index

Note: Boldface page numbers indicate illustrations.

Patricia D. Netzley has written more than fifty books for children, teens, and adults. She has also worked as an editor, a writing instructor, and a knitting teacher. She is a member of the Society of Children's Book Writers and Illustrators.